FALL LEAVES

By Cliff Griswold

Gareth Stevens
PUBLISHING

Please visit our website, www.garethstevens.com. For a free color catalog of all our high-quality books, call toll free 1-800-542-2595 or fax 1-877-542-2596.

Library of Congress Cataloging-in-Publication Data

Griswold, Cliff.
 Fall leaves / Cliff Griswold.
     pages cm. — (Fun in fall)
 Includes index.
 ISBN 978-1-4824-1777-7 (pbk.)
 ISBN 978-1-4824-1778-4 (6 pack)
 ISBN 978-1-4824-1776-0 (library binding)
 1. Autumn—Juvenile literature. 2. Fall foliage—Juvenile literature. I. Title. II. Series: Griswold, Cliff. Fun in fall.
 QB637.7.G75 2015
 575.5'7—dc23
                                            2014022972

First Edition

Published in 2015 by
Gareth Stevens Publishing
111 East 14th Street, Suite 349
New York, NY 10003

Copyright © 2015 Gareth Stevens Publishing

Editor: Ryan Nagelhout
Designer: Nicholas Domiano

Photo credits: Cover, p.1 Asia Images/Asia Images/Getty Images; p. 5 Bonita R. Cheshier/Shutterstock.com; p. 7 Artens/Shutterstock.com; p. 9 Digital Media Pro/Shutterstock.com; p. 11 StevenRussellSmithPhotos/Shutterstock.com; pp. 13, 24 (leaves) ntdanai/Shutterstock.com; p. 15 S.Borisov/Shutterstock.com; p. 17 Mny-Jhee/Shutterstock.com; pp. 19, 24 (tree) SP-Photo/Shutterstock.com; pp. 21, 24 (rake) Ariel Skelley/Blend Images/Getty Images; p. 23 Julie DeGuia/Shutterstock.com.

Printed in the United States of America

CPSIA compliance information: Batch #CW15GS: For further information contact Gareth Stevens, New York, New York at 1-800-542-2595.

Contents

I love fall.
It is also called autumn.

The trees change color in fall.

7

Green leaves
will change to
something new.

Fall leaves are many different colors.

Some leaves are yellow.

13

Others change to red.

The leaves start to fall.

Our trees are
now bare!

I help my mom
rake the leaves.
I use a green rake.

My sister jumps
into the pile of leaves!

Words to Know

leaves

rake

tree

Index